Exploring Money

Needs and Wants

by Connor Stratton

FOCUS READERS®
PIONEER

www.focusreaders.com

Copyright © 2023 by Focus Readers®, Lake Elmo, MN 55042. All rights reserved. No part of this book may be reproduced or utilized in any form or by any means without written permission from the publisher.

Focus Readers is distributed by North Star Editions:
sales@northstareditions.com | 888-417-0195

Produced for Focus Readers by Red Line Editorial.

Photographs ©: Shutterstock Images, cover (left), cover (center), cover (right), 1 (left), 1 (center), 1 (right), 4, 6 (top), 6 (bottom), 8, 10, 12, 14 (bottom), 17, 18, 21; iStockphoto, 14 (top)

Library of Congress Cataloging-in-Publication Data
Names: Stratton, Connor, author.
Title: Needs and wants / by Connor Stratton.
Description: Lake Elmo, MN : Focus Readers, [2023] | Series: Exploring money | Includes index. | Audience: Grades 2-3
Identifiers: LCCN 2022006602 (print) | LCCN 2022006603 (ebook) | ISBN 9781637392393 (Hardcover) | ISBN 9781637392911 (Paperback) | ISBN 9781637393949 (PDF) | ISBN 9781637393437 (eBook)
Subjects: LCSH: Money--Juvenile literature. | Budget--Juvenile literature | Finance, Personal--Juvenile literature. | Basic needs--Juvenile literature.
Classification: LCC HG221.5 .S78 2023 (print) | LCC HG221.5 (ebook) | DDC 332.4--dc23/eng/20220302
LC record available at https://lccn.loc.gov/2022006602
LC ebook record available at https://lccn.loc.gov/2022006603

Printed in the United States of America
Mankato, MN
082022

About the Author

Connor Stratton writes and edits nonfiction children's books. Growing up, he helped his dad collect the 50 State Quarters.

Table of Contents

CHAPTER 1
Needs 5

CHAPTER 2
Wants 9

CHAPTER 3
Spending Money 13

THAT'S AMAZING!
Meeting All Needs 16

CHAPTER 4
Making a List 19

Focus on Needs and Wants • 22
Glossary • 23
To Learn More • 24
Index • 24

Chapter 1

Needs

All people have certain needs. People need food and water. They need safe shelter. People need clothing, too. Without these things, people cannot **survive**.

Other things are also very important. People might need health care. They might need transportation. Education matters a lot, too.

Some people keep extra food and water at home.

Chapter 2

Wants

People also have many wants. They might want certain **goods**. A girl might want a new phone. Or she might want ice cream. The girl can live without ice cream. But she enjoys the taste.

Other wants are **services**. One day, someone might want a haircut. The next day, that person might want to go out to eat.

Did You Know? Some things that people want are costly. People must **save** money to buy them.

Chapter 3

Spending Money

Most needs and wants are not free. People must **spend** money for these things. But people can run out of money.

Suppose a boy has $30. He pays $10 for a toy. Then he rips his pants. He needs a new pair. But new pants cost $25. The boy can't **afford** them. He has only $20 left. He did not **manage** his money.

Did You Know? People work at jobs to get money. Then, they can spend it or save it.

That's Amazing!

Meeting All Needs

Usually, people have to pay for all their basic needs. But some people do not earn enough money. Many places are trying to fix this problem. Some places provide free housing. Others provide free health care. And others offer free food to people.

Chapter 4

Making a List

People can make lists of their needs and wants. They write how much those things cost. People also write how much money they have. Then they subtract the cost of their needs.

Next, people see how much money is left over. That money can go toward something they want. Or they can save the money for later.

Did You Know? People often make **budgets**. That helps them keep track of their money.

Wants	Needs
New Shoes $50	Groceries $100
Haircut $30	Winter Coat $50
Book $10	Medicine $30

FOCUS ON
Needs and Wants

Write your answers on a separate piece of paper.

1. Write a sentence that explains the main idea of Chapter 4.

2. What are some of your wants and needs? How do you get them?

3. What is an example of a need?
    - A. toy
    - B. phone
    - C. water

4. Suppose you need a $10 meal and want a $7 toy. You have $15. How much more money would you need to buy both things?
    - A. $2
    - B. $3
    - C. $5

Answer key on page 24.

Glossary

afford
To have enough money to pay for something.

budgets
Tools that help people keep track of how much they save and spend.

goods
Items people can buy.

manage
To handle or control something.

save
To set money aside so it can be used later.

services
Actions of helping or doing work for others.

spend
To use money to pay for something.

survive
To continue to live or exist.

To Learn More

BOOKS

Huddleston, Emma. *Managing Money*. Lake Elmo, MN: Focus Readers, 2021.

Ventura, Marne. *Needs and Wants*. Minneapolis: Abdo Publishing, 2018.

NOTE TO EDUCATORS

Visit **www.focusreaders.com** to find lesson plans, activities, links, and other resources related to this title.

Index

B
budgets, 20

C
cost, 11, 15, 19

G
goods, 9

S
save, 11, 15, 20
services, 11

Answer Key: 1. Answers will vary; 2. Answers will vary; 3. C; 4. A